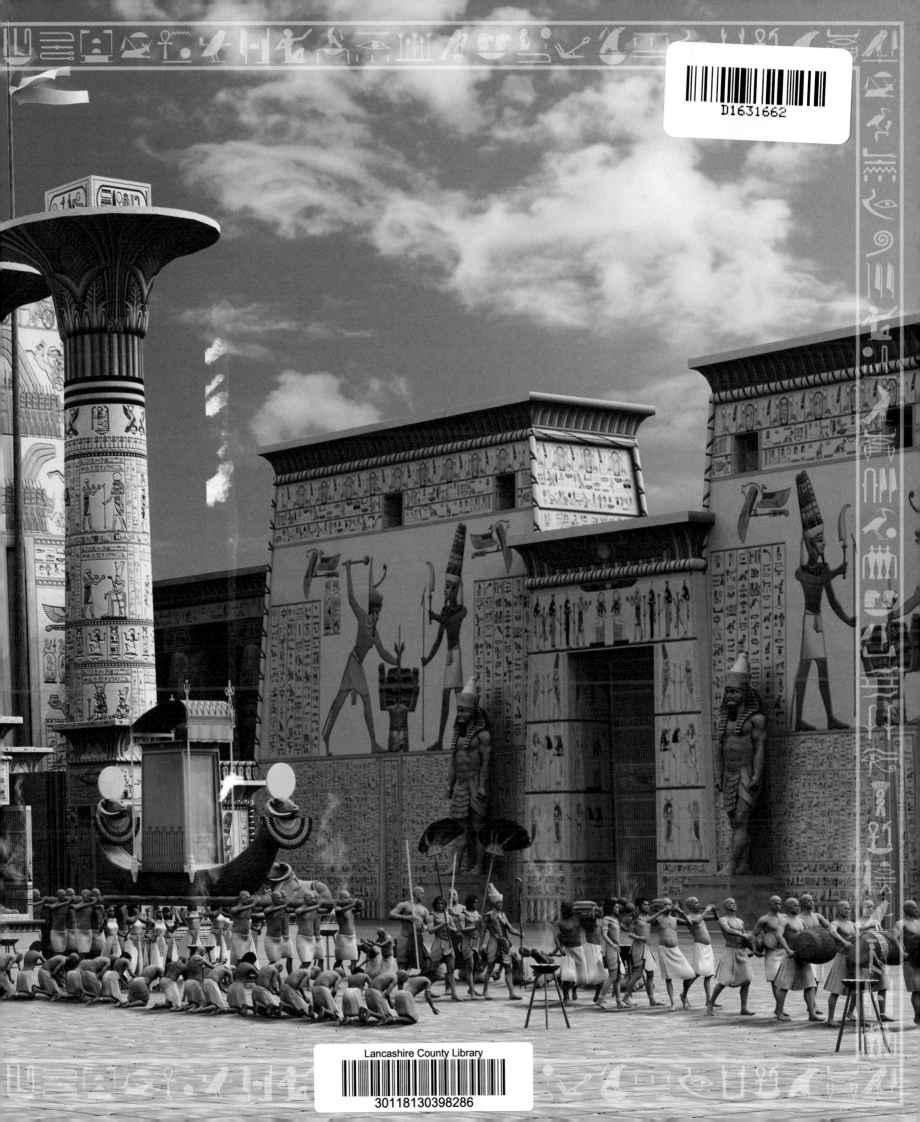

Egyptworld

DISCOVER THE WONDERS
OF THE ANCIENT LAND OF TUTANKHAMUN
AND CLEOPATRA

STELLA CALDWELL

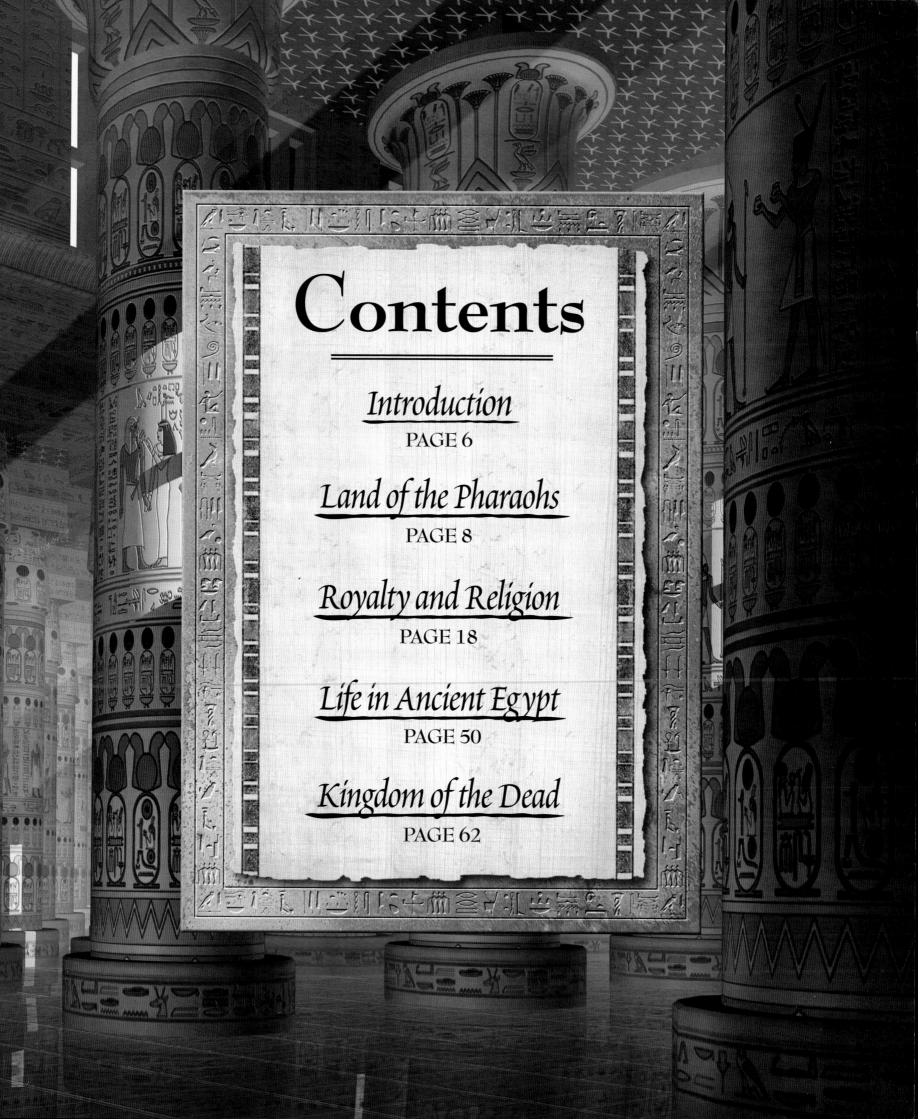

Contents

I GREW UP HEARING tales of my great-great grandfather James Caldwell. He was an adventurer who had spent a year exploring Egypt in the 1870s. Later, I recalled snatches of what I'd heard as a child – of how James had once been present when a mummy was raised from its ancient resting place – and stories too of long-held secrets and forgotten treasures.

It was not until my father's death that I first came across James's journal. Yellowed and torn, it had lain forgotten in a dusty attic for decades. Reading of his extraordinary journey aboard a wooden dahabeeyah – an Egyptian house boat – from Alexandria to Abu Simbel, I sensed the raw excitement he had felt in discovering that ancient land.

However, it was James's account of a chance meeting with a man named Ahmed Abdel Rassoul that caught my attention. It is now well known that around the 1870s, the Abdel Rassoul brothers stumbled across a hidden tomb high above the ruins of Hatshepsut's temple. Within they discovered royal mummies and fantastic riches. Keeping the tomb a secret from the authorities, they set about selling its treasures in local markets.

Incredibly, James's journal records that he was one such buyer. I was stunned – where were these objects now? Feverishly, I set about searching the attic – a difficult task, for it was crammed with the belongings of three generations – and eventually came across a small metal box. Inside, wrapped up in heavy cloth, were several objects: a jewelled bracelet glinting with the eye of Horus, two beautifully crafted figures and a fragile scrap of papyrus.

6

– 2 –

James lived during a time when excitement at Egypt's newly discovered history ran high. He was wrong to have taken these treasures and the objects are now back where they belong in Cairo. However, I cannot forget the thrill of holding them, nor the sense that for a brief moment history came alive in my hands. You will find them displayed here amongst the pages of this book, a tribute to my ancestor and to all those who have sought to uncover the secrets of the ancient Egyptians.

Stella Caldwell
– OXFORD

Land of the Pharaohs

Our last weeks upon the Nile have passed in a haze of burning heat. The temperature rises daily — buffalo stand up to their necks in the shallows and occasionally we glimpse basking crocodiles. As we draw near to Cairo, I must pause to reflect upon this most extraordinary of journeys. For although I had read much of this astonishing land, nothing could have prepared me for the wonder of seeing it with my own eyes. There is the harsh beauty of the desert and the endless charms of this remarkable river. But it is the magnificent ruins — the beautiful temples and mysterious tombs — that have constantly thrilled me for these past months.

James Caldwell

10th May 1874

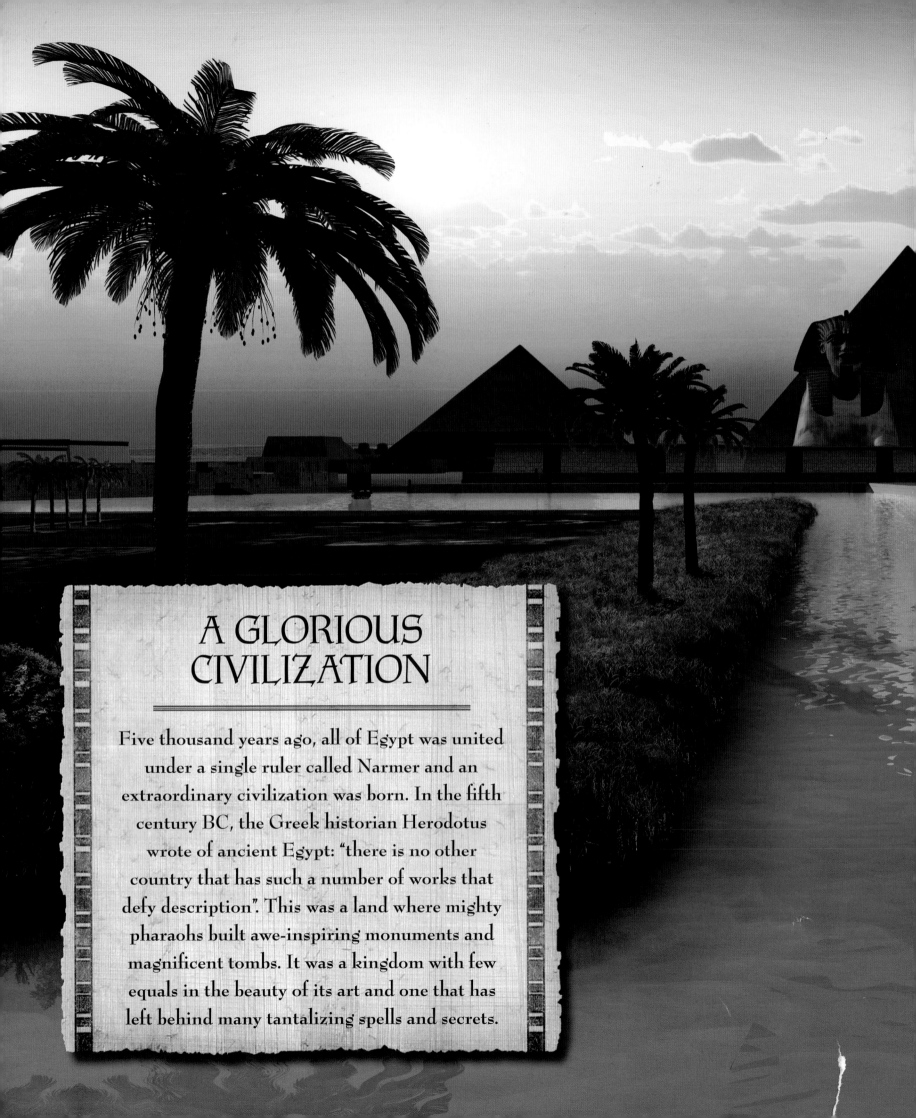

A GLORIOUS CIVILIZATION

Five thousand years ago, all of Egypt was united under a single ruler called Narmer and an extraordinary civilization was born. In the fifth century BC, the Greek historian Herodotus wrote of ancient Egypt: "there is no other country that has such a number of works that defy description". This was a land where mighty pharaohs built awe-inspiring monuments and magnificent tombs. It was a kingdom with few equals in the beauty of its art and one that has left behind many tantalizing spells and secrets.

KINGDOMS AND DYNASTIES

Throughout its long history, ancient Egypt was ruled by a succession of pharaohs, or kings. An early historian divided them into ruling families or "dynasties", a system that is still in use today. Rulers were usually, though not always, blood relatives. The Dynastic Age lasted for over 3,000 years, from around 3000 BC to the death of Egypt's last pharaoh, Cleopatra VII, in 30 BC.

OLD KINGDOM
(c. 2686–2181 BC) DYNASTIES 3–6

For the first time, whole monuments began to be constructed in stone. This was the age of pyramids, with the Great Pyramids and the Sphinx being built at Giza.

3000 BC

2000 BC

PREDYNASTIC PERIOD
(c. 5000–3000 BC)

During this period, people lived in small settlements along the Nile. Egypt was divided into two kingdoms, Upper and Lower Egypt.

FIRST INTERMEDIATE PERIOD
(c. 2181–2055 BC) DYNASTIES 7–11

This was a period of chaos and instability. Ancient texts speak of "70 kings in 70 days", for rulers quickly came and went.

EARLY DYNASTIC PERIOD
(c. 3000–2686 BC) DYNASTIES 1–2

Upper and Lower Egypt were united for the first time, with Memphis as the capital city. Early hieroglyphic writing appeared and the first tombs, known as mastaba tombs, were built.

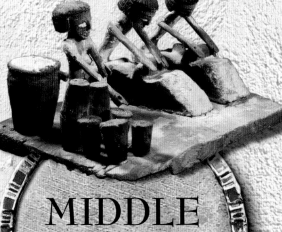

MIDDLE KINGDOM
(c. 2055–1650 BC)
DYNASTIES 11–14

Ancient Egypt was now stable and this was a period of great creativity, with art and literature flourishing. The pharaohs ruled from Itj-Tawy, a city that has now completely disappeared.

NEW KINGDOM
(c. 1550–1069 BC) DYNASTIES 18–20

With the Hyksos now driven out of Egypt, this was the start of a golden age. Egypt's empire became large and powerful, with rulers based at the city of Thebes. Pharaohs were now buried in rock-cut tombs in the Valley of the Kings.

LATE PERIOD
(c. 715–332 BC) DYNASTIES 25–30

During this unsettled period, foreign kings from Nubia and Persia mainly ruled Egypt. Alexander the Great of Macedon conquered Egypt in 332 BC.

13

1000 BC

SECOND INTERMEDIATE PERIOD
(c. 1650–1550 BC)
DYNASTIES 15–17

Egypt again fell into a period of chaos. Foreigners from the east began to arrive in the Nile Delta – the Egyptians called them Hyksos. These invaders gradually became more powerful, until they controlled most of Egypt.

THIRD INTERMEDIATE PERIOD
(c. 1069–715 BC) DYNASTIES 21–24

Egypt's days of glory were coming to an end. The power of the pharaohs dwindled and a period of confusion and division began.

PTOLEMAIC PERIOD
(c. 332–30 BC) PTOLEMAIC DYNASTY

This Macedonian Greek royal family ruled Egypt for nearly 300 years from the city of Alexandria. The death of Cleopatra VII marked the end of Egypt's Dynastic Age.

THE RIVER OF LIFE

Herodotus, a Greek historian writing in the fifth century BC, called Egypt "the gift of the Nile", for without the river there would have been no great civilization in Egypt. In the summer of every year the Nile flooded, leaving behind a rich black mud that fertilized the land. We now know that the river flooded because it was swollen by rains far away in Ethiopia, but the ancient Egyptians believed that this seemingly miraculous event was the work of the gods.

THE BLACK LAND

The ancient Egyptians called their country Kemet, the Black Land, because of the fertile soil that lay along either side of the Nile. Vegetables and fruit, such as onions, grapes and pomegranates, grew in abundance. The river teemed with fish and was also home to hippos and crocodiles. Wildfowl nested in the riverside marshes, while animals such as antelopes and gazelles grazed on the edge of the floodplain. Away from the Black Land was the vast desert known as Deshret or the Red Land, one of the driest regions on Earth.

RIGHT *The importance of river boats in ancient Egypt is clear from the number of model boats – such as this one – that have been found in tombs.*

14

ABOVE Oxen pull a plough as the soil is prepared for planting crops. The land fertilized by the Nile was perfect for growing grains such as wheat and barley.

RIGHT Papyrus paper was made from the stems of papyrus reeds (left) that grew along the banks of the Nile. Our word "paper" comes from the word "papyrus".

BELOW This painting from a tomb wall shows workers picking grapes, which grew in large quantities along the Nile.

ANCIENT EGYPT

This map was found in James Caldwell's journal and outlines his voyage from Alexandria to Abu Simbel. It is not a detailed map of the country, but shows the most important features of ancient Egypt and a few of James's observations. The all-important Nile carved out the geography of Egypt as it flowed from south to north. The Nile Valley was known as Upper Egypt, while to the north was Lower Egypt where the Nile branched out to form the Nile Delta.

Deir el-Bahri

It is difficult to imagine a more lovely temple than that built by the female pharaoh Hatshepsut.

LOWER EGYPT

Cairo

Memphis

Amarna (Akhetaten)

Giza

The sight of this desert cemetery is hard to describe – huge Pyramids and the colossal statue of the Sphinx shut out the sky.

Alexandria

My journey began at this ancient port. Cleopatra VII died here in 30BC.

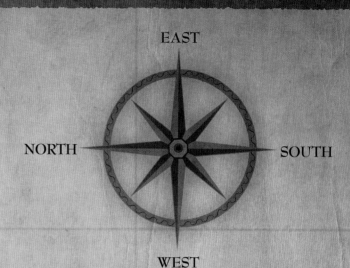

EAST

NORTH   SOUTH

WEST

Karnak

The derelict ruins of the largest temple on Earth are still awe-inspiring.

Edfu

The temple here was dedicated to the falcon-headed god Horus.

UPPER EGYPT

Luxor (Thebes)

Ramesseum

Ramesses II's majestic temple, where giant statues now lay broken on the sands.

Valley of the Kings

The hidden valley where New Kingdom pharaohs were buried.

Abu Simbel

The furthermost point of my voyage. This is where the temples of Ramesses II stand carved from rock – a truly extraordinary sight!

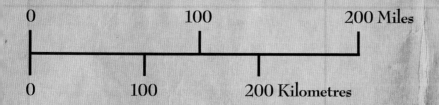

0   100   200 Miles

0   100   200 Kilometres

Royalty and Religion

We have now been at Abu Simbel for five days and this morning made a wonderful discovery. We had taken donkeys to the edge of the desert and were ascending a rocky slope on foot. By chance, a crack running down a rock face caught our guide's eye – poking a stick into the opening, he became convinced that a space lay hidden behind it. For many hours we toiled in the burning sun, scraping away at the sand. By sunset, there was an opening just wide enough for me to squeeze through and taking a candle, I was astonished to find myself peering down into a small painted chamber. Feverishly I called out to the others, for we had surely stumbled upon the entrance to a tomb...

James Caldwell

22nd December 1873

THE MIGHTY PHARAOHS

More than just a ruler, the pharaoh was believed to be a "god-king" filled with the divine power of the falcon-headed god Horus. In total, there were around 170 pharaohs in Ancient Egypt; most of them ruled with supreme authority, though they were still expected to abide by the principles of justice and mercy, or ma'at as it was known. The pharaoh's chief wife and queen played an important role in court life. Only very rarely did women become pharaohs themselves. The most famous of these were Hatshepsut, who ruled Egypt for about 20 years, and Egypt's last pharaoh, Cleopatra VII.

ABOVE *The falcon-headed god Horus leads Queen Nefertari by the hand. All pharaohs were believed to be filled with Horus's spirit.*

GODS AND KINGS

The Egyptians believed that in the beginning Egypt was ruled by the gods, who lived on Earth like people. The sky god Horus was king of the living, while Osiris was god of the dead. When the gods ceased to rule on Earth, Horus sent his spirit to enter the pharaoh. When a king died, it was believed that he became one with Osiris in the afterlife, while the spirit of Horus passed on to the next ruler.

LEFT *Ramesses II, one of Egypt's most famous pharaohs, ruled Egypt for over 90 years. He is often referred to as Ramesses the Great.*

SYMBOLS OF POWER

In Egyptian art, pharaohs are usually shown holding a shepherd's crook and a flail (a tool used for threshing corn). These symbols represent the pharaoh's power as protector of his people and the fertility of the land. Kings were often shown with a gold cobra headdress, a gold collar and a false beard. On ceremonial occasions, pharaohs wore a variety of crowns. The red crown represented Lower Egypt, the white crown Upper Egypt and the double crown combined the two. By the New Kingdom, the bright blue khepresh crown had appeared, which reflected the pharaoh's importance as a warrior.

THE RULE OF EGYPT

Although the pharaoh had absolute power in Egypt, he was assisted by ministers who carried out important duties. Below the king were two viziers for Upper and Lower Egypt, and the Viceroy of Kush who governed Nubia. The viziers had responsibility for government departments and the justice system. Beneath the viziers were the army and the priesthood, along with officials who looked after areas such as the Treasury and building projects.

RIGHT *Thutmose III was a great leader and brilliant general, who conquered more land than any other pharaoh.*

HATSHEPSUT

Hatshepsut was one of ancient Egypt's most successful rulers. During her 20-year reign, this pharaoh built splendid temples and successfully defended Egypt's borders. However, very soon after her death in 1457 BC, her monuments were pulled down and her name was erased from history. It would be over 3,000 years before her story was rediscovered.

ABOVE *Hatshepsut's beautiful mortuary temple, named the Holy of Holies, was vandalized after her death.*

A QUEEN BECOMES KING

Queen Hatshepsut's rise to power was extraordinary. She was the wife and queen of Thutmose II; they had no sons together, so when the king died, power passed to the queen's stepson, another Thutmose. However, he was still a baby and, as was the custom, Hatshepsut was expected to rule Egypt until Thutmose was old enough to take control. However, within a few years the queen had seized power and declared herself pharaoh. She was crowned and began to dress like a male pharaoh, even wearing a false beard.

LEFT *This statue of Hatshepsut shows her wearing the traditional false beard of a male pharaoh and was a symbol of her absolute power.*

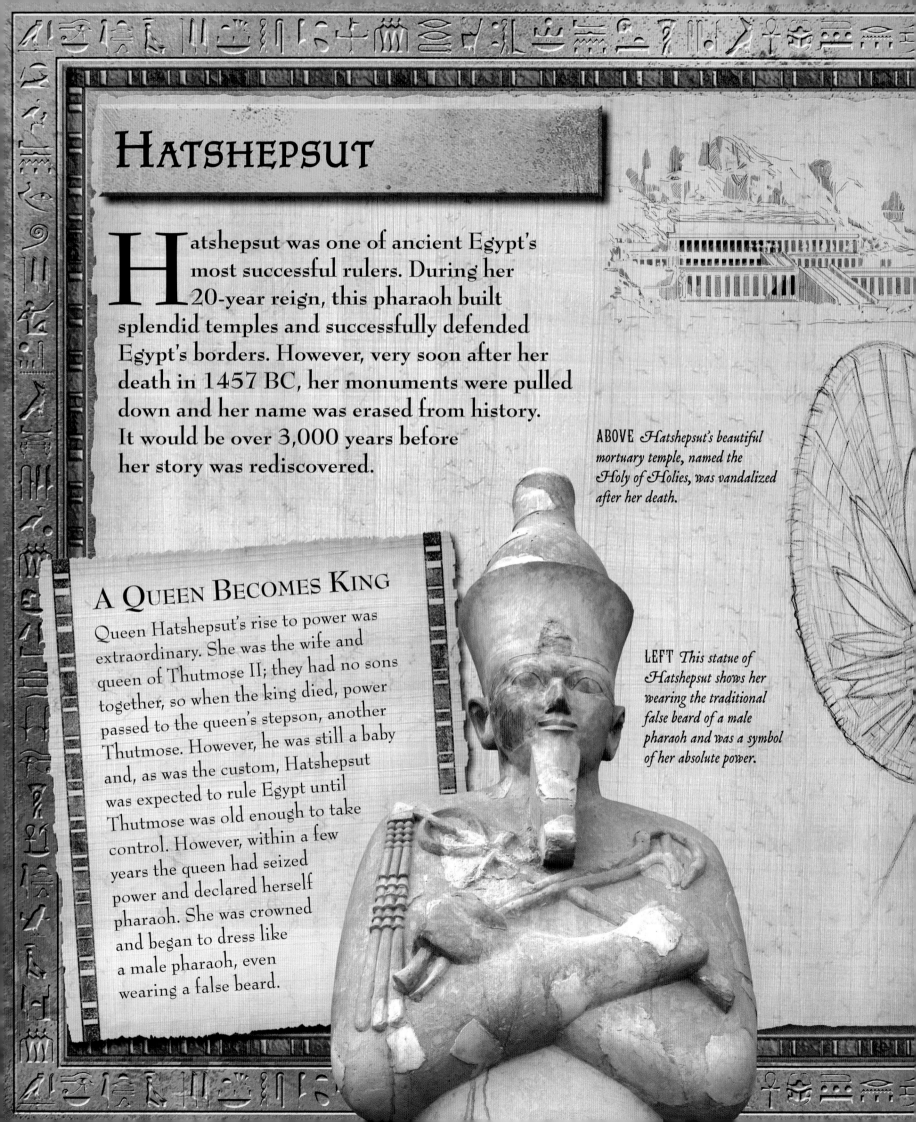

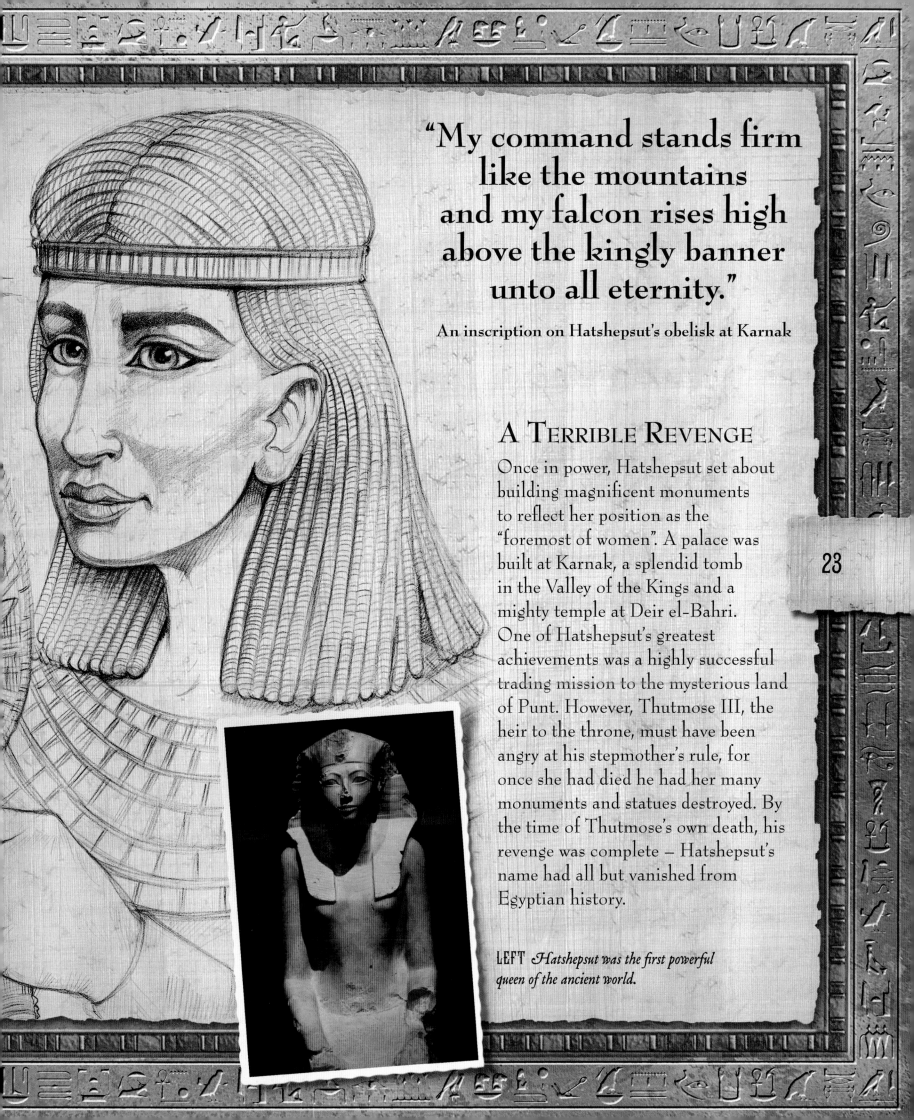

> "My command stands firm like the mountains and my falcon rises high above the kingly banner unto all eternity."

An inscription on Hatshepsut's obelisk at Karnak

A TERRIBLE REVENGE

Once in power, Hatshepsut set about building magnificent monuments to reflect her position as the "foremost of women". A palace was built at Karnak, a splendid tomb in the Valley of the Kings and a mighty temple at Deir el-Bahri. One of Hatshepsut's greatest achievements was a highly successful trading mission to the mysterious land of Punt. However, Thutmose III, the heir to the throne, must have been angry at his stepmother's rule, for once she had died he had her many monuments and statues destroyed. By the time of Thutmose's own death, his revenge was complete – Hatshepsut's name had all but vanished from Egyptian history.

LEFT *Hatshepsut was the first powerful queen of the ancient world.*

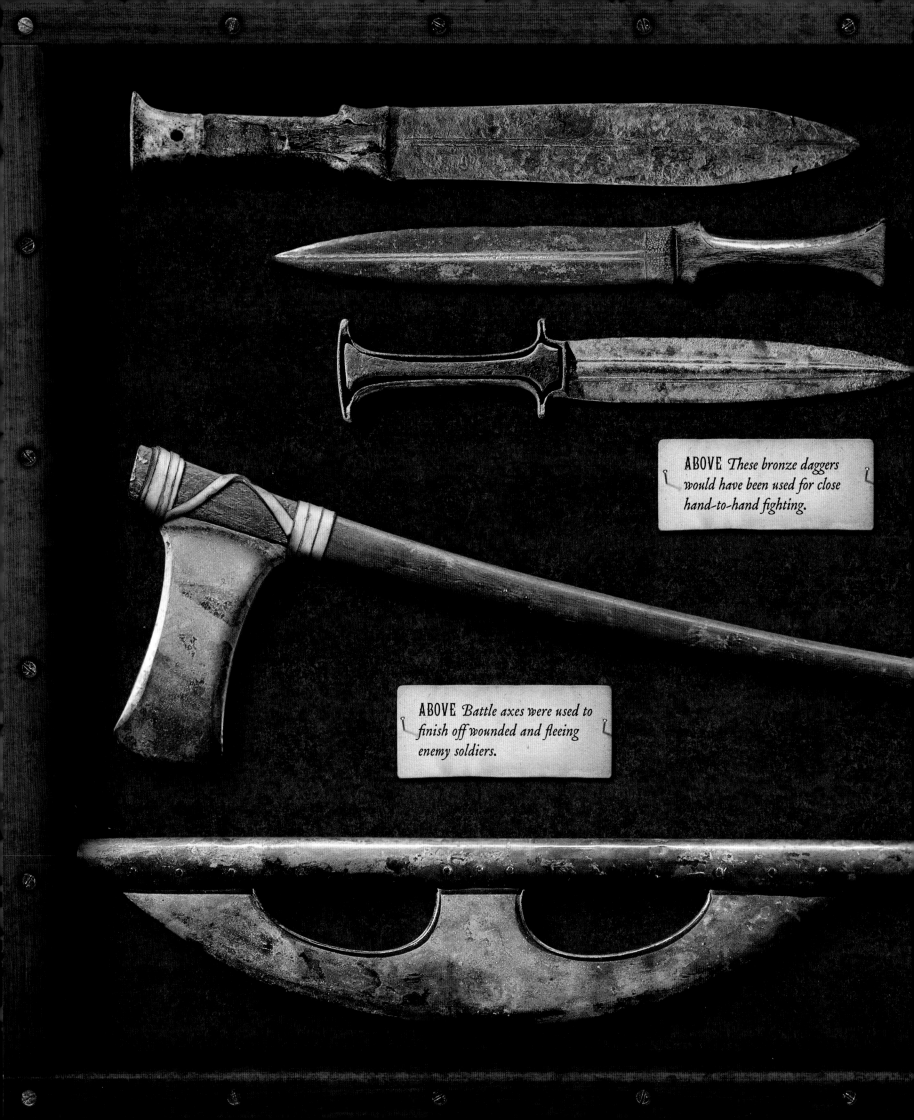

ABOVE *These bronze daggers would have been used for close hand-to-hand fighting.*

ABOVE *Battle axes were used to finish off wounded and fleeing enemy soldiers.*

EGYPT AT WAR

For more than a thousand years, Egypt's sea and desert were enough to prevent invasion and there was no need for a fully equipped army. By the time of the New Kingdom, however, Egypt's army had grown to become an impressive fighting force. Elite soldiers rode swiftly into battle in horse-drawn chariots. Foot soldiers carrying long leather shields were armed with spears, battle axes and daggers, while archers fired bronze or flint-tipped arrows. Captured prisoners sometimes had a hand cut off to prevent them fighting again. Following one of Ramesses III's victories over the Libyans, thousands of hands were piled into a mound and presented to the pharaoh as battle trophies.

BELOW *The bow and arrow let soldiers in war chariots swiftly attack from a distance.*

RIGHT *Bronze-headed spears like this one could be thrown or thrust at enemy soldiers.*

ABOVE *The long, sharpened blade of this axe would have had a lethal slicing action.*

GODS AND MYTHS

Across their 3,000-year history, the ancient Egyptians worshipped hundreds of gods and goddesses. Some early gods disappeared altogether, while others developed into new gods. Important gods, such as the sun god Ra, were worshipped throughout Egypt. Others, such as the cat goddess Bastet, were only worshipped in certain areas. Ancient Egypt had many myths and even the best known of these had several different versions.

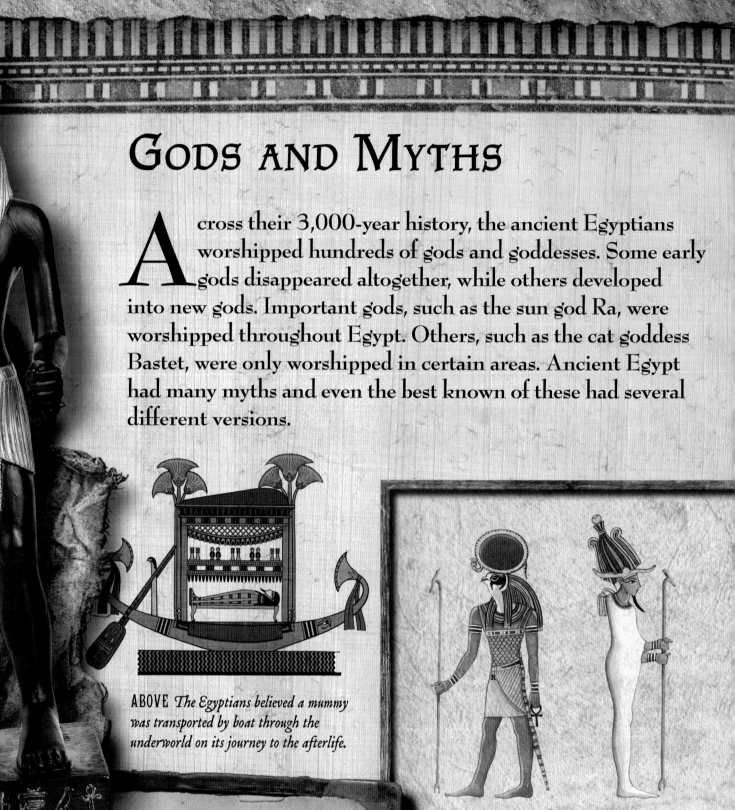

ABOVE *The Egyptians believed a mummy was transported by boat through the underworld on its journey to the afterlife.*

RA was the most important god and represented the sun. He was believed to rule all creation.

OSIRIS was god of the dead. His underworld kingdom was thought to look like Egypt.

Statue

I have bought a statue of the jackal-headed god the Egyptians called Anubis, friend and protector of the dead. Thousands of years have not dulled its gleaming splendour, and I shiver to think of this very figure silently keeping watch over a pharaoh's mummy since ancient times...

James Caldwell

Cairo, 15th August 1874

OSIRIS, THE FIRST MUMMY

The ancient Egyptians told the story of how Osiris once ruled Egypt as a good king. However, his jealous brother Seth tricked him into climbing into a coffin and threw him into the Nile. The king's heartbroken wife Isis found Osiris's corpse and hid it, but Seth discovered her secret and cut his brother's body up, scattering the pieces across Egypt. Turning herself into a bird of prey, Isis soared high above the land and found all but one of the body parts. With the help of the gods Anubis and Thoth, the parts were wrapped in cloth and laid out in the shape of Osiris. Isis kissed the mummy and Osiris was reborn to live forever as king of the dead in the underworld.

ABOVE *In later times the sun god Ra was joined with Horus as the god Ra-Horakhty (centre).*

ISIS was the wife of Osiris, and was worshipped as the goddess of nature and fertility.

HORUS was the son of Osiris and Isis, and was god of the sky. His spirit entered Egypt's pharaohs.

ANUBIS was the jackal-headed god of mummies who watched over funeral rites.

THOTH was the god of wisdom and patron of scribes. He was pictured as either an ibis bird or a baboon.

SETH was Osiris's evil brother and the god of darkness and chaos.

AKHENATEN

The rule of Akhenaten is one of the strangest and most puzzling episodes in Egyptian history. Crowned Amenhotep IV sometime around 1353 BC, this "heretic pharaoh" swept away Egypt's traditional gods in favour of a single god called Aten and changed his name to Akhenaten ("servant of the Aten").

THE NEW RELIGION

The old gods had watched over Egypt for 2,000 years, but Akhenaten banned their worship at a single stroke. Temples were adapted to worship the new god Aten and the names of earlier gods were removed from inscriptions. A new capital city was built in honour of Aten called Akhetaten, a site today known as Amarna. Images of Akhenaten and his family show them as having strangely long heads and big hips. Some Egyptologists believe that this style of art was connected to the new religion, while others have suggested that perhaps the family suffered from a form of inherited disease.

RIGHT *Akhenaten, Nefertiti and their daughters worship the Aten. This god was always portrayed as a sun with rays reaching downwards.*

LEFT *Akhenaten saw himself as the living form of the god Aten.*

ABOVE *Nefertiti helped her husband to set up Egypt's new religion. However, after they had died, their names became hated throughout the land.*

QUEEN NEFERTITI

Akhenaten's closest assistant was his chief wife Nefertiti (above) whose beauty was legendary. What became of Nefertiti is a mystery, however, for in the twelfth year of the king's rule, her name vanished from history. Akhenaten's successor Smenkhkare is a mysterious figure too. Some doubt his existence, while others believe he may actually have been Nefertiti ruling under a new name.

AKHETATEN DESERTED

Akhenaten's new religion did not survive his death. Under the reign of Smenkhkare's successor, Tutankhamun, the city of Akhetaten was abandoned and gradually crumbled back into desert. Thebes was once again declared Egypt's capital and the old gods were restored.

Mummies and Tombs

The ancient Egyptians believed that every person was made up of five elements: a name (ren), a soul (ba), a life force (ka), a shining form (akh) and a shadow (sheut). In order to be reborn in the afterlife, these all needed to be reunited with the body. This is why the Egyptians took such care in preparing for death and went to great trouble to preserve the dead body as a mummy.

Making a Mummy

The first Egyptian mummies occurred naturally. Bodies were buried in the hot, dry sand of the desert, conditions that prevented rotting because the bacteria that cause decay were unable to survive. As society developed and wealthy Egyptians began to be buried in coffins and tombs, people looked for another way to preserve the body. Embalming and mummification, a process that took 70 days to carry out, was developed over hundreds of years. It was skilled and gruesome work, but it worked. Many superbly preserved New Kingdom mummies have been discovered, demonstrating how successful the technique was.

RIGHT *Anubis, the god of embalming and "friend of the dead", stands over an embalmed pharaoh.*

LEFT *Animals associated with gods were mummified too. This cat mummy might have been offered to the cat goddess Bastet.*

30

1. A slit was made in the left side of the body and the stomach, lungs, intestines and liver removed. These organs were embalmed and placed in four pottery jars (above). The heart, believed to be the centre of intelligence, was left in the body. The brain, considered unimportant, was removed through the nose and thrown away.

2. Embalmers then covered the body with a salt called natron, which soaked up moisture and prevented decay. The body was left to dry out for 40 days. It was then stuffed with materials soaked in oils and resins to return it to a normal shape.

3. The body was now wrapped in linen layers. This took 15 days. Jewels and amulets (charms) believed to have magical powers were placed between the layers of linen strips to protect the person in the afterlife.

4. A mask was placed over the mummy's head before it was laid in a coffin, often with a portrait of the dead person on the lid. The coffins of important people might be human-shaped and have several richly-decorated layers.

31

MUMMY MYSTERIES

The technique of embalming was extremely effective. However, it made the flesh of mummies look horribly withered and the pressure of the linen wrappings could cause much damage, especially to the nose. The mummies of many pharaohs have been uncovered, but identifying who's who can be difficult. Experts look for facial similarities between family members and can even analyse a mummy's DNA, although this is complex and challenging work.

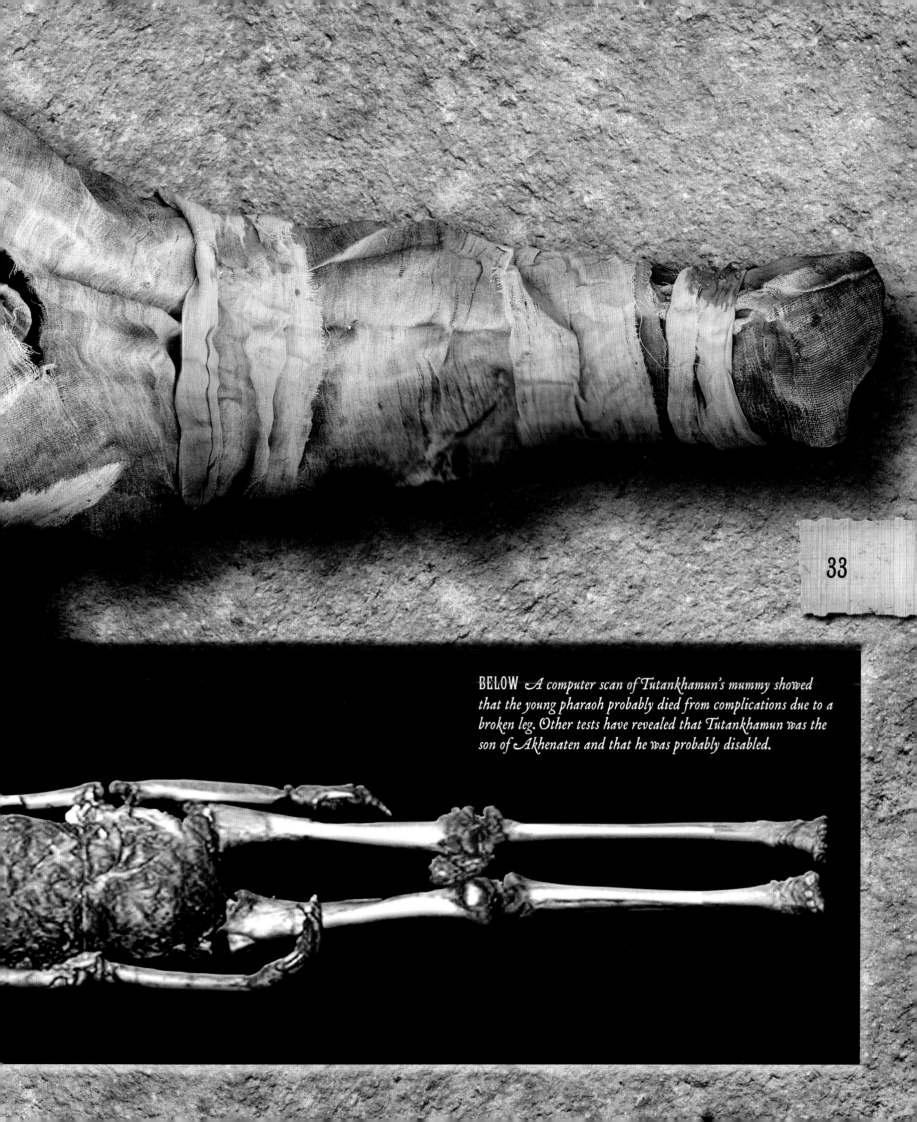

33

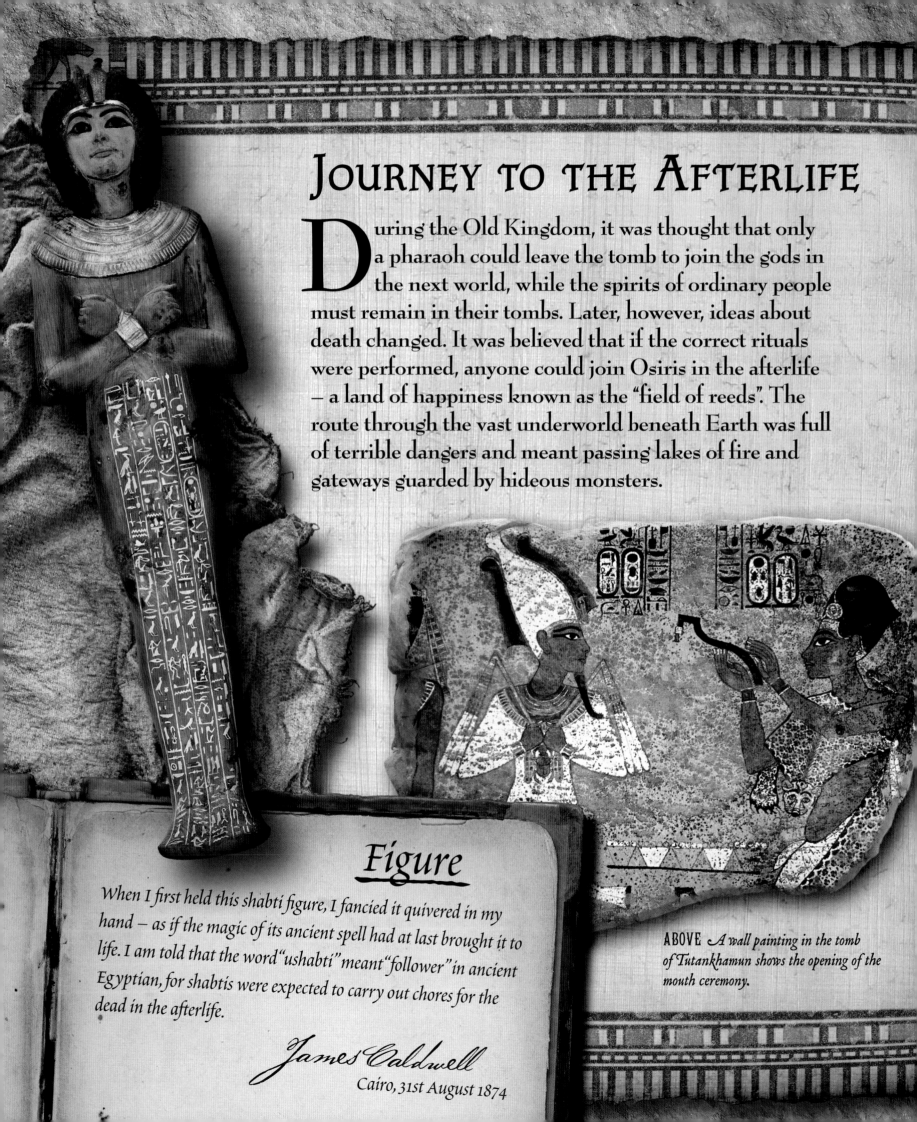

JOURNEY TO THE AFTERLIFE

During the Old Kingdom, it was thought that only a pharaoh could leave the tomb to join the gods in the next world, while the spirits of ordinary people must remain in their tombs. Later, however, ideas about death changed. It was believed that if the correct rituals were performed, anyone could join Osiris in the afterlife — a land of happiness known as the "field of reeds". The route through the vast underworld beneath Earth was full of terrible dangers and meant passing lakes of fire and gateways guarded by hideous monsters.

Figure

When I first held this shabti figure, I fancied it quivered in my hand — as if the magic of its ancient spell had at last brought it to life. I am told that the word "ushabti" meant "follower" in ancient Egyptian, for shabtis were expected to carry out chores for the dead in the afterlife.

James Caldwell
Cairo, 31st August 1874

ABOVE *A wall painting in the tomb of Tutankhamun shows the opening of the mouth ceremony.*

Servants for the Field of Reeds

Ancient Egyptians worried that they might be expected to work in the afterlife. For this reason, wealthy people were often buried with small shabti figures. It was thought that these model servants, inscribed with a spell that allowed them to spring to life when needed, would be able to perform the tasks instead.

The Opening of the Mouth Ceremony

During an Egyptian funeral, female mourners were hired to weep and wail for the dead person. The coffin was carried to the tomb where the mummy was placed in an upright position and a priest performed the important "opening of the mouth ceremony". The mouth was touched with sacred tools, thus allowing the soul to return to life. The coffin was then placed in the tomb surrounded by items that would be needed in the afterlife, such as food and furniture and the tomb was then sealed.

ABOVE *In later times it became common for 401 shabtis to be included in each burial – one "worker" for each day of the year, plus an extra shabti for each group of ten.*

BELOW *The god Anubis weighs the heart of a dead person against Ma'at, represented by a feather of truth.*

The Book of the Dead

Magic spells to protect a dead person against the dangers of the underworld were often inscribed on coffins. Spells were also written on tomb walls or on scrolls of papyrus – these texts are now called The Book of the Dead. It held the key to surviving the voyage through the underworld. The most important test awaited in the Hall of Two Truths, where a person's heart was weighed against Ma'at, the goddess of truth. If it was judged too heavy, Ammit, "Devourer of the Dead", swallowed the heart and the person would not be allowed to continue their journey.

A SPELL
FOR THE DEAD

This manuscript comes from a papyrus scroll of The Book of the Dead found in the tomb of a man named Hunefer (shown below with his wife Nasha). A royal scribe, Hunefer lived in Thebes around 3,000 years ago. The spell shown here is a hymn to the rising sun and is written in hieroglyphs. At the bottom right, the goddesses Nephthys and Isis summon Osiris, god of the dead, back to life.

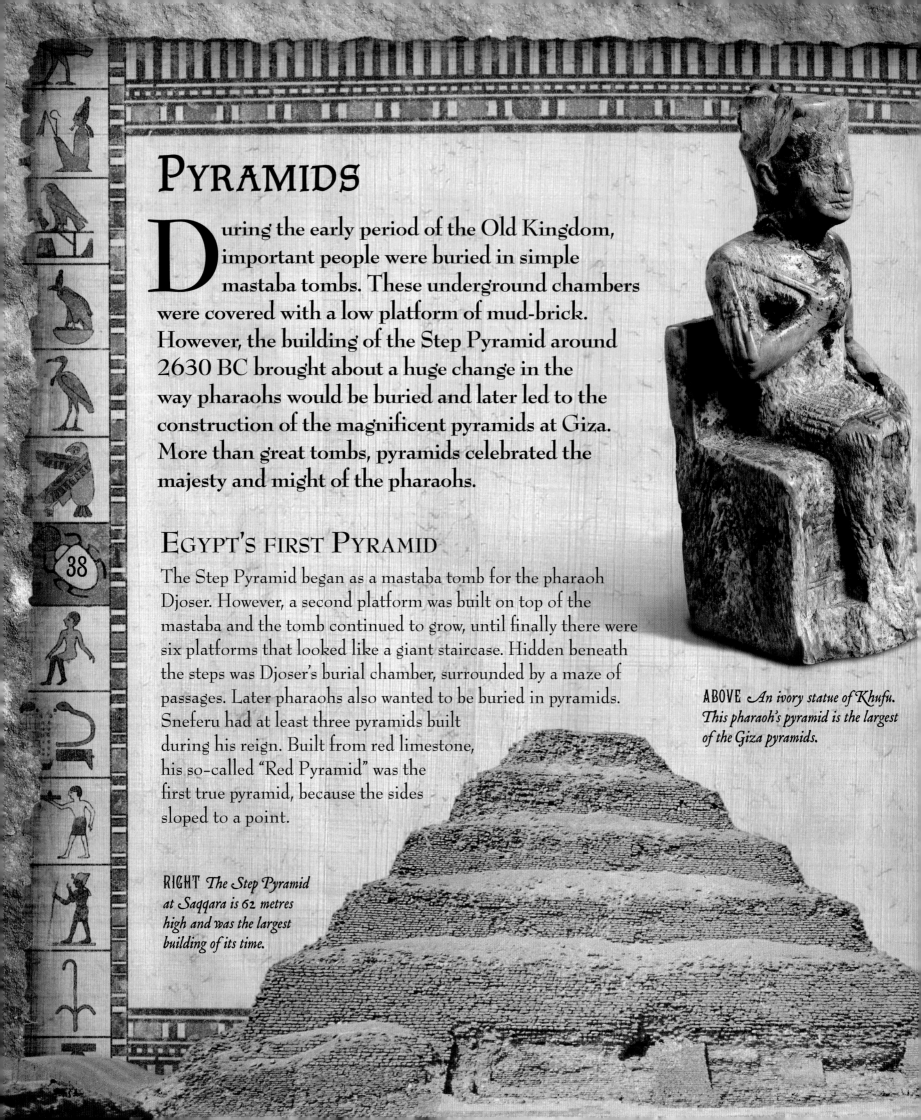

PYRAMIDS

During the early period of the Old Kingdom, important people were buried in simple mastaba tombs. These underground chambers were covered with a low platform of mud-brick. However, the building of the Step Pyramid around 2630 BC brought about a huge change in the way pharaohs would be buried and later led to the construction of the magnificent pyramids at Giza. More than great tombs, pyramids celebrated the majesty and might of the pharaohs.

EGYPT'S FIRST PYRAMID

The Step Pyramid began as a mastaba tomb for the pharaoh Djoser. However, a second platform was built on top of the mastaba and the tomb continued to grow, until finally there were six platforms that looked like a giant staircase. Hidden beneath the steps was Djoser's burial chamber, surrounded by a maze of passages. Later pharaohs also wanted to be buried in pyramids. Sneferu had at least three pyramids built during his reign. Built from red limestone, his so-called "Red Pyramid" was the first true pyramid, because the sides sloped to a point.

ABOVE *An ivory statue of Khufu. This pharaoh's pyramid is the largest of the Giza pyramids.*

RIGHT *The Step Pyramid at Saqqara is 62 metres high and was the largest building of its time.*

LEFT *This photograph taken from space clearly shows the three pyramids at Giza. Satellite images are now helping archaeologists to uncover Egypt's lost pyramids.*

THE GREAT PYRAMID

Even today, the Giza pyramids built for the pharaohs Khufu, his son Khafre and grandson Menkaure have the power to fill us with awe. The ancient Greeks and Romans considered Khufu's Great Pyramid – the largest of the three – to be one of the Seven Wonders of the Ancient World and it is still the largest stone building on Earth. Built from around 2.3 million blocks of stone, each weighing 2.5 tonnes, Khufu's pyramid is 147 metres tall. Inside, the pyramid is riddled with tunnels and chambers. Khufu was buried within the pyramid itself rather than in an underground chamber. Although his sarcophagus remains in place, tomb-robbers stole its contents long ago.

1. Underground burial chamber
2. Queen's chamber
3. King's chamber
4. Air shafts
5. Weight-relieving chambers
6. Grand gallery
7. Vents
8. Entrance

BELOW *A cross-section of the Great Pyramid. The underground chamber may have been the original king's chamber or perhaps it was there to trick robbers.*

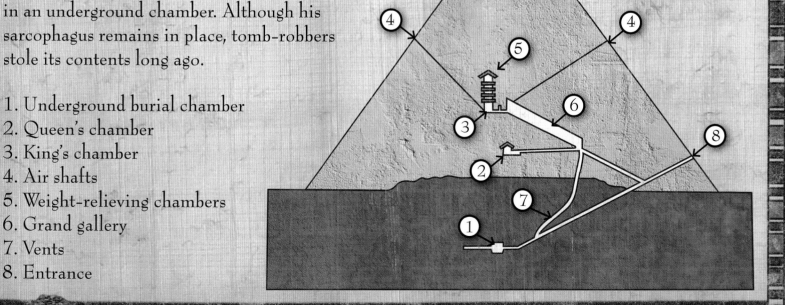

The Pyramids

It is hard to describe my feelings on first viewing the Pyramids, for their extraordinary size eclipses everything. How exactly they were built remains a mystery, though surely ramps of some form must have been used. I am told that in ancient times, all three pyramids had temples and were covered in shimmering limestone. One can only imagine the glorious sight of these wonders glinting in the desert sun…

The Great Sphinx

Standing solemn and silent in the desert, a strange beast with the head of a pharaoh and the body of a lion stares out towards the rising sun. Locals tell me this giant sculpture near Khafre's pyramid was carved from a single ridge of stone, and was once colourfully painted. Thousands of years of wind and sand have eroded the Sphinx's mighty face, but I still shivered to gaze upon it . . .

THE VALLEY OF THE KINGS

Tomb robbers looted the pyramids of Old and Middle Kingdom pharaohs soon after their funerals, so during the New Kingdom a new tradition began. For nearly 500 years, almost all pharaohs were buried in secret rock-cut tombs in the Valley of the Kings. Set deep in dramatic cliffs, the valley lies across the Nile from Luxor (once the ancient city of Thebes). However, despite the valley's remote situation, only the tomb of Tutankhamun escaped being completely ransacked by thieves.

44

ABOVE *The wives of pharaohs were buried close to their husbands in the Valley of the Queens. This wall painting from the tomb of Nefertari, a wife of Ramesses II, shows her playing the game Senet.*

LEFT *The Valley of the Kings was chosen for its isolated location, but tomb robbers were still able to loot almost all the pharaohs' tombs.*

A TOMB MYSTERY

In 1817, the magnificent tomb of the pharaoh Seti I was discovered by Giovanni Battista Belzoni. The longest of any tomb in the Valley of the Kings, its narrow passageways and many chambers are beautifully decorated. However, the reason for a mysterious tunnel that descends deep into the rock below has long puzzled Egyptologists. In 2010, it was discovered that the passage comes to a sudden end, its final step unfinished. Could it be that Seti I intended another burial chamber to be built – a secret tomb within a tomb – but died before the work could be completed? It seems likely the secret died with this great pharaoh, and so the mystery remains.

ABOVE *A detail from the beautifully painted tomb of Seti I, showing the pharaoh with the god Ra-Horakhty.*

BELOW *An early diagram of Seti I's tomb. Its tunnel is the longest of any in the Valley of the Kings.*

Spaccato del sepolcro
e della cappella ,oggi
in rovina, ricostruita
nel disegno

The Great Temples

Along the banks of the Nile stood magnificent temples dedicated to the worship of important gods. Each temple site was believed to be the dwelling place of a god, so new temples were simply built upon the foundations of old ones. The splendid temple of Amun-Re at Thebes – now called Karnak – is the biggest of all the temples still standing in Egypt.

ABOVE *A massive statue of Ramesses II from his rock-cut temple at Abu Simbel.*

Temple Rituals

Although much of Egyptian life revolved around the temples, only pharaohs and priests could worship within them. An outer wall surrounded each temple with a main gate leading into the courtyard. This was as far as ordinary people could go and then only during special festivals. Beyond this point, the temple grew increasingly dark until the tiny sanctuary containing the god's shrine was reached. Here, sacred rituals were carried out three times a day. Priests entered the sanctuary to wash and dress the god's statue, applying perfumes and eye-paint. Incense was burned and food and drink were offered. At night, priests swept away their footsteps as they left, so as to remove all human traces.

RIGHT *The beautifully preserved Temple of Horus at Edfu was built during Egypt's Ptolemaic period.*

46

THE COLOSSI OF MEMNON

At the side of a road leading to the Valley of the Kings, two gigantic statues tower over the landscape. These are the Colossi of Memnon and once guarded the temple of the pharaoh Amenhotep III, which later kings pulled down for its stone. In 27 BC, an earthquake apparently cracked one of the statues and it began to make an eerie moaning noise at dawn. This was probably an effect of the rising sun's warmth on the stone, but the ancient Greeks claimed they were hearing the sighs of King Memnon, a hero of the Trojan War. In 199 AD, the Romans carried out repairs to the statue, and the Colossus has remained silent ever since.

BELOW *The massive seated figures of Amenhotep III are all that remain of this pharaoh's temple.*

ABOVE *Priests used ceremonial vessels like this one during temple rituals.*

Karnak Temple

Even in its crumbling condition, Karnak filled me with awe — one can only imagine what a splendid sight this giant temple complex must have been in ancient times. Here is the first court of the Temple of Amun. Where only a single column stands today, there were once 10 massive pillars built by the pharaoh Taharqa. As I stood amongst the silent ruins, I tried to imagine the rituals once carried out within these sacred walls...

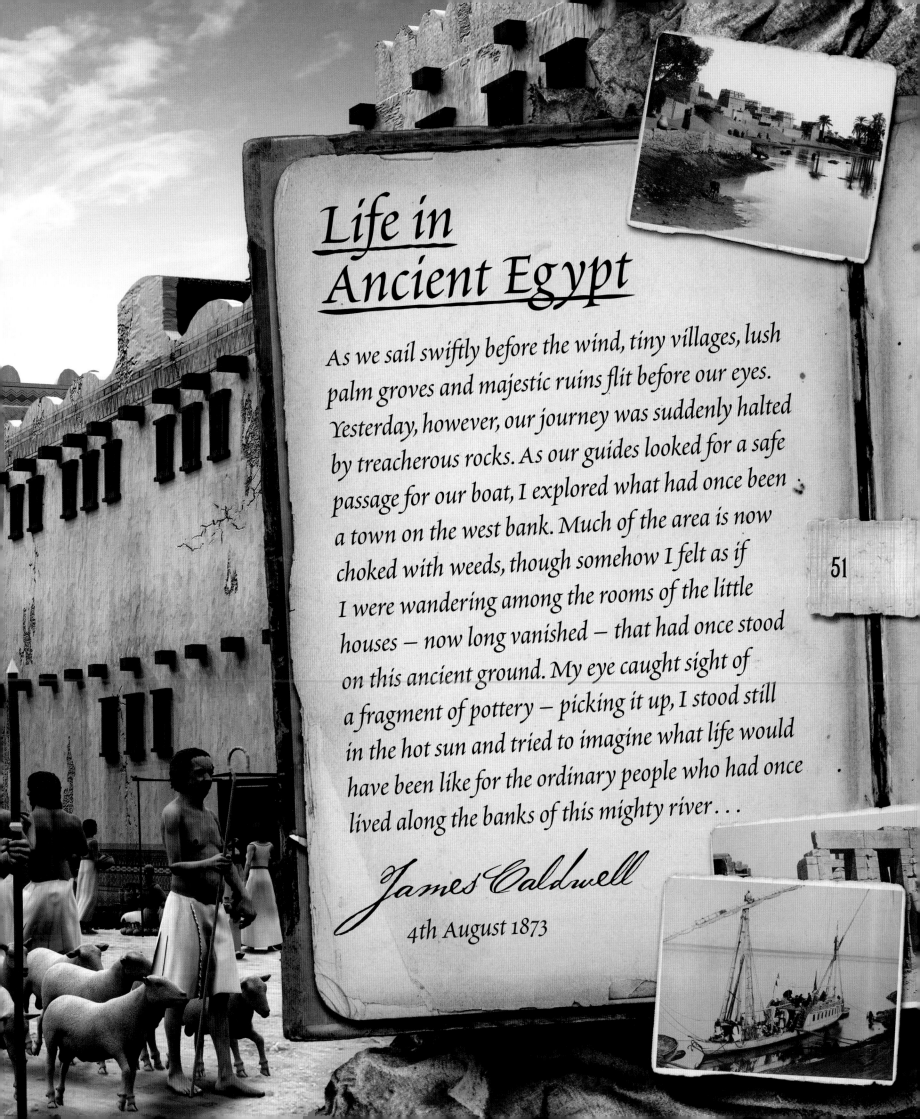

Life in Ancient Egypt

As we sail swiftly before the wind, tiny villages, lush palm groves and majestic ruins flit before our eyes. Yesterday, however, our journey was suddenly halted by treacherous rocks. As our guides looked for a safe passage for our boat, I explored what had once been a town on the west bank. Much of the area is now choked with weeds, though somehow I felt as if I were wandering among the rooms of the little houses – now long vanished – that had once stood on this ancient ground. My eye caught sight of a fragment of pottery – picking it up, I stood still in the hot sun and tried to imagine what life would have been like for the ordinary people who had once lived along the banks of this mighty river...

James Caldwell

4th August 1873

An Egyptian Home

Temples and monuments were built of stone, but Egyptian homes were made of less durable mud-brick. This is why so few ordinary houses have survived. Much of our knowledge of them comes from tomb paintings and models. The yearly Nile flood meant there was never a shortage of mud. Combined with straw, the mud was poured into wooden moulds to make bricks that were baked in the hot desert sun. Houses were whitewashed to reflect the sun's heat and were cool and dark inside.

ABOVE *This vessel in the form of a woman carrying a vase dates from around 3,500 years ago.*

Rich and Poor

The poorest Egyptians lived in cramped one-room houses. Furniture was a luxury – those who could afford it had low chairs and tables made from local wood and beds made of mud brick. In the towns, space was very scarce and houses were built two or three storeys high. Household waste was emptied into pits and the river, or simply dropped from windows. People spent a lot of time on the roof to keep cool in the breeze and to escape the smells of the dirty streets below. Rich Egyptians lived in luxurious villas with many different rooms and furniture made from expensive imported wood. Villas often had pretty gardens and pools stocked with fish.

LEFT *A model of a typical Egyptian home dating from around 4,000 years ago.*

RIGHT *The homes of the wealthy often had beautiful gardens.*

52

DEIR EL-MEDINA

When the New Kingdom pharaohs began building royal tombs in the Valley of the Kings, a village for workmen and their families was built nearby at Deir el-Medina. Preserved beneath the desert sands for 3,500 years, its ancient remains were discovered in the 1920s. Seventy narrow houses were crammed together and enclosed by a thick wall – these homes all had an entrance hall, living and sleeping areas, and a kitchen at the back. Wall shrines contained statues of gods and dead family members. The workers also built their own tombs, usually consisting of a small chapel and an underground chamber covered by a small pyramid.

ABOVE *The ruins at Deir el-Medina have much to tell us about everyday Egyptian life.*

BELOW *A chair and broom found at Deir el-Medina.*

53

Food and Feasting

The ancient Egyptians loved good food and wine, and enjoyed a varied diet. Bread and beer were made from wheat and barley and farmers grew many vegetables and fruits. The Nile provided plentiful fish and meats such as goat and pork were common. Beef, however, was a luxury, as only rich people could afford to keep cattle.

An Egyptian Party

Scenes from tomb wall-paintings show that the Egyptians loved parties. The rich held extravagant banquets, serving delicacies like roasted quail and goose, pigeon stew and sweet honey cakes, along with wine and beer. As the guests ate their fill, musicians played on instruments such as harps and lyres. Afterwards it was the turn of singers, dancers and acrobats to perform. As well as making merry, the Egyptians also enjoyed relaxing and playing board games. Everyone, from pharaohs to farmers played the game of Senet, a bit like the modern-day game of backgammon. Tutankhamun was buried with four senet boards, including a magnificent board made from ebony and ivory.

ABOVE *This lady plucking a harp is a detail from a larger banquet scene painted on a tomb wall.*

HUNTING

While hunting and fishing provided food for many Egyptians, richer people hunted for sport. Wild bulls, gazelles and lions were all hunted in the desert. King Amenhotep III claimed to have killed over 100 lions in 10 years! Throwing sticks were used to hunt birds, while nets made from reeds and papyrus were used to trap both birds and fish. The most dangerous sport was hunting crocodiles and hippos – teams of hunters harpooned them, before dragging them ashore with ropes and nets.

DAILY BREAD

Bread was an important part of the Egyptian diet, but it often contained grit from the stones used to grind flour. Many mummies have shown that the coarse bread caused the Egyptians' teeth to wear away – even mighty pharaohs would have suffered from terrible toothache.

ABOVE *This beautiful tomb painting shows a scribe named Nebamun hunting birds in the marshes of the Nile.*

LEFT *Instruments such as this drum were an important part of Egyptian life – no celebration was complete without music and dancing.*

ABOVE *This beautiful wooden comb needed to be sturdy as wig hair could be long and heavy.*

FASHION AND FINERY

The ancient Egyptians loved beauty and took great care over their appearance. Clothing was usually made of cool white linen and varied from simple dresses to beautifully decorated robes. Many shaved their heads and wore fancy wigs made from human hair. Both men and women highlighted their eyes with heavy eyeliner. The Egyptians covered themselves with jewellery in life and death. The rich wore magnificent gold and silver pieces, often set with semi-precious stones. Poorer Egyptians wore jewellery made from cheaper materials such as copper or a glazed ceramic called faience.

LEFT *This snake ring dates from around the time when Cleopatra VII was pharaoh.*

Bracelet

What pharaoh's arm was adorned by this exquisite bracelet? The Eye of Horus – an ancient Egyptian symbol granting safety from evil – gazes out from it. It was believed that Horus's all-seeing eyes were the sun and the moon, and this symbol was used to protect both the living and the dead.

James Caldwell

Cairo, 31st August 1874

ABOVE *Elaborate beaded bracelets and necklaces were very popular with the Egyptians.*

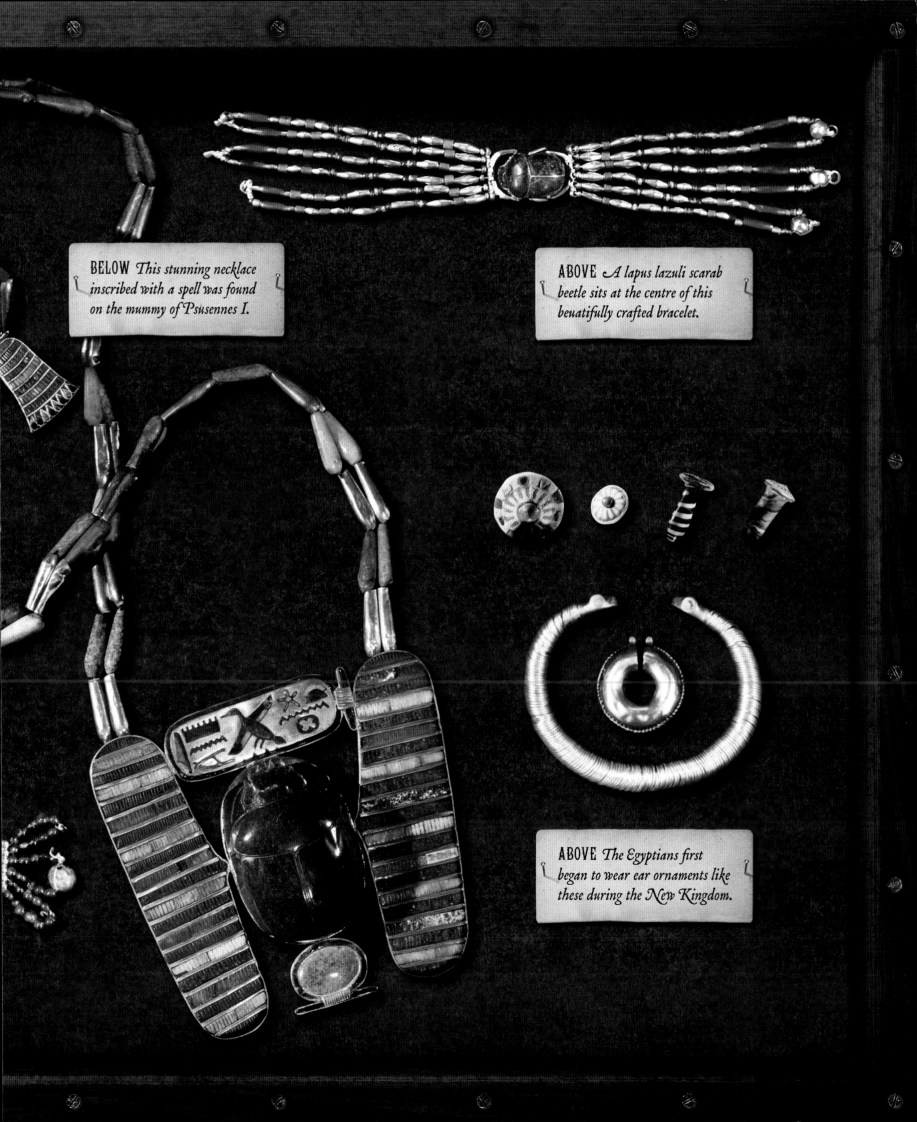

BELOW *This stunning necklace inscribed with a spell was found on the mummy of Psusennes I.*

ABOVE *A lapus lazuli scarab beetle sits at the centre of this beuatifully crafted bracelet.*

ABOVE *The Egyptians first began to wear ear ornaments like these during the New Kingdom.*

Ramesses the Great

Ramesses II is often regarded as the most powerful of all ancient Egypt's kings. Ruling for 67 years and fathering well over 100 children, Ramesses's magnificent monuments were built to ensure that his name would be never be forgotten.

RIGHT Ramesses fought bravely at the Battle of Kadesh, the largest chariot battle in history.

Remembered In Stone

Ramesses left behind many extraordinary monuments such as the Ramesseum, his vast temple near Thebes and the hypostyle hall at Karnak. However, his greatest building project was the magnificent rock-cut temples at Abu Simbel carved out of a cliff face above the Nile. The Great Temple of Ramesses was created with such incredible accuracy that at sunrise on one day in February and one day in October, the sun shines through the entrance to light up three of the great statues of the gods.

The Warrior King

Ramesses II was trained for battle from an early age. In the fifth year of his reign, this warrior king gathered a mighty army to attack the Hittites in what is now Syria. The Egyptians camped outside the city of Kadesh, but unknown to Ramesses the enemy was lying in wait and the pharaoh marched his soldiers straight into a trap. Although hugely outnumbered, Ramesses encouraged his men to fight bravely on and the Hittites were held off. Eventually both armies withdrew exhausted and in time a peace treaty – the first in history – was signed. Despite the fact that there was no clear winner, the pharaoh celebrated the Battle of Kadesh as a great victory on temple walls throughout Egypt.

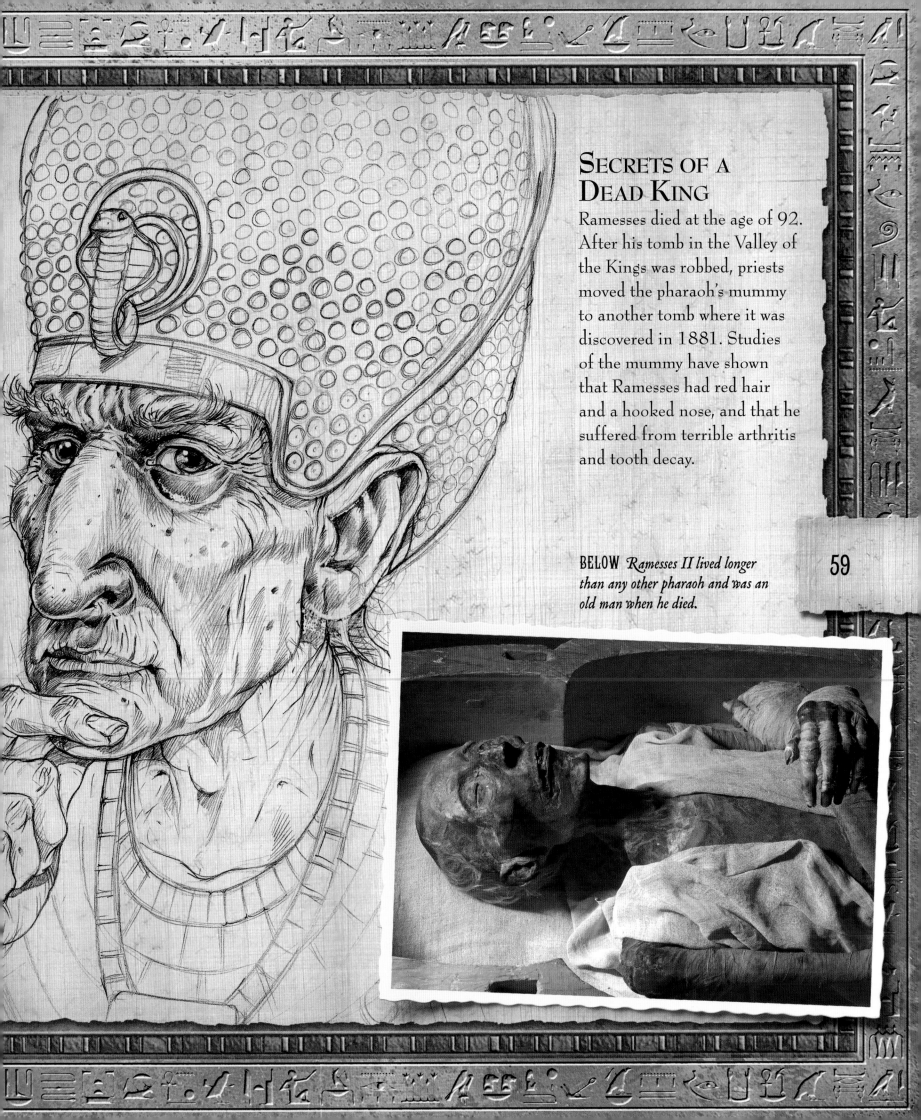

SECRETS OF A DEAD KING

Ramesses died at the age of 92. After his tomb in the Valley of the Kings was robbed, priests moved the pharaoh's mummy to another tomb where it was discovered in 1881. Studies of the mummy have shown that Ramesses had red hair and a hooked nose, and that he suffered from terrible arthritis and tooth decay.

BELOW *Ramesses II lived longer than any other pharaoh and was an old man when he died.*

59

Boats of the Nile

As the mighty Nile slowly carries us south, I have often imagined what this bustling river looked like in ancient times. Early Egyptians used small boats made from papyrus reeds, but later all sorts of craft busied these waters, from small wooden rowing boats to swift sailboats and huge cargo ships. It is truly astonishing to think of these giant vessels transporting heavy stone blocks to building sites like the Pyramids, and even bearing the weight of entire obelisks.

Kingdom of the Dead

Yesterday we were invited to watch the opening of a newly discovered tomb. Setting out at dawn, we crossed the river by boat and then went on donkey-back. Before us the massive statues of the Colossi of Memnon towered up against the sky, glinting in the morning light. Workers were already hard at work digging when we arrived, and I shall never forget my excitement as the shape of something buried beneath the sand gradually appeared. The men dropped their picks and spades, and scraped with their bare hands — and then a painted mummy case rose to the surface. The coffin was heaved upright and placed on the edge of the pit, and I shivered to think of the mummy that lay inside, undisturbed for all these thousands of years . . .

James Caldwell

14th February 1874

EGYPT'S SECRETS REVEALED

For hundreds of years, people struggled to make sense of Egypt's ancient history. Without being able to read the mysterious writing known as hieroglyphs, it was impossible for explorers to know why monuments had been built or by whom. Then, in 1798, Napoleon's soldiers discovered a slab of black stone at a place called Rosetta on the Mediterranean coast. It had three scripts on it: one in Greek and two in Egyptian. At last, here was the key to Egypt's long-lost ancient language.

ABOVE *Champollion, the man who unlocked hieroglyphs, is often called the Father of Egyptology.*

CRACKING THE CODE

It was Jean-François Champollion who finally translated the three scripts on the Rosetta Stone in 1822. Building on the work of earlier scholars, the Frenchman was able to show that most hieroglyphs stand for sounds and he found the letters of our alphabet that roughly match up. Other hieroglyphs stand for whole words. Champollion also discovered that special names, such as those of the pharaohs, were often contained in oval shapes called "cartouches".

Papyrus

This scrap of papyrus, long entombed with a dead king, surely comes from The Book of the Dead. It is possible to make out the terrible figure of the monster known as Ammit, Devourer of the Dead. The Egyptians believed this dreadful demon consumed the souls of those refused entry to the afterlife.

James Caldwell

Cairo, 31st August 1874

BELOW *The statues from the Abu Simbel temples were lifted up the cliff face, away from rising waters.*

Treasure Seekers

Once people were able to read hieroglyphs, many adventurers excitedly began to explore ancient sites. In 1818, Giovanni Battista Belzoni – an ex-circus man – removed the colossal bust of Ramesses II from the Ramesseum and had it shipped to England where it remains to this day. It was only later in the century that more careful excavation methods came about. For example, William Flinders Petrie realized that tiny fragments had as much to tell us about Egypt's past as large monuments and he began to carefully record all his finds.

Preserving the Past

The study of ancient Egypt isn't just about making new discoveries – equally important is the work of making sure that objects and sites are properly preserved. In the 1960s, an extraordinary conservation project took place after the Aswan High Dam was built to control Egypt's water supply. This dam would have flooded the beautiful temples at Abu Simbel, so they were cut into blocks and moved to safety, 65 metres up the cliff face.

65

THE ROSETTA STONE

The text on this block of carved granite is repeated in three different scripts. The first 14 lines are hieroglyphs, the middle section is "demotic" (a shortened version of hieroglyphs) and the last 54 lines are in Greek. Champollion realized that the scripts were translations of each other and by comparing them was able to work out two royal names: Ptolemy and Cleopatra. From here he was able to find hieroglyphs for all the Greek words and the secret of Egypt's ancient language was unlocked.

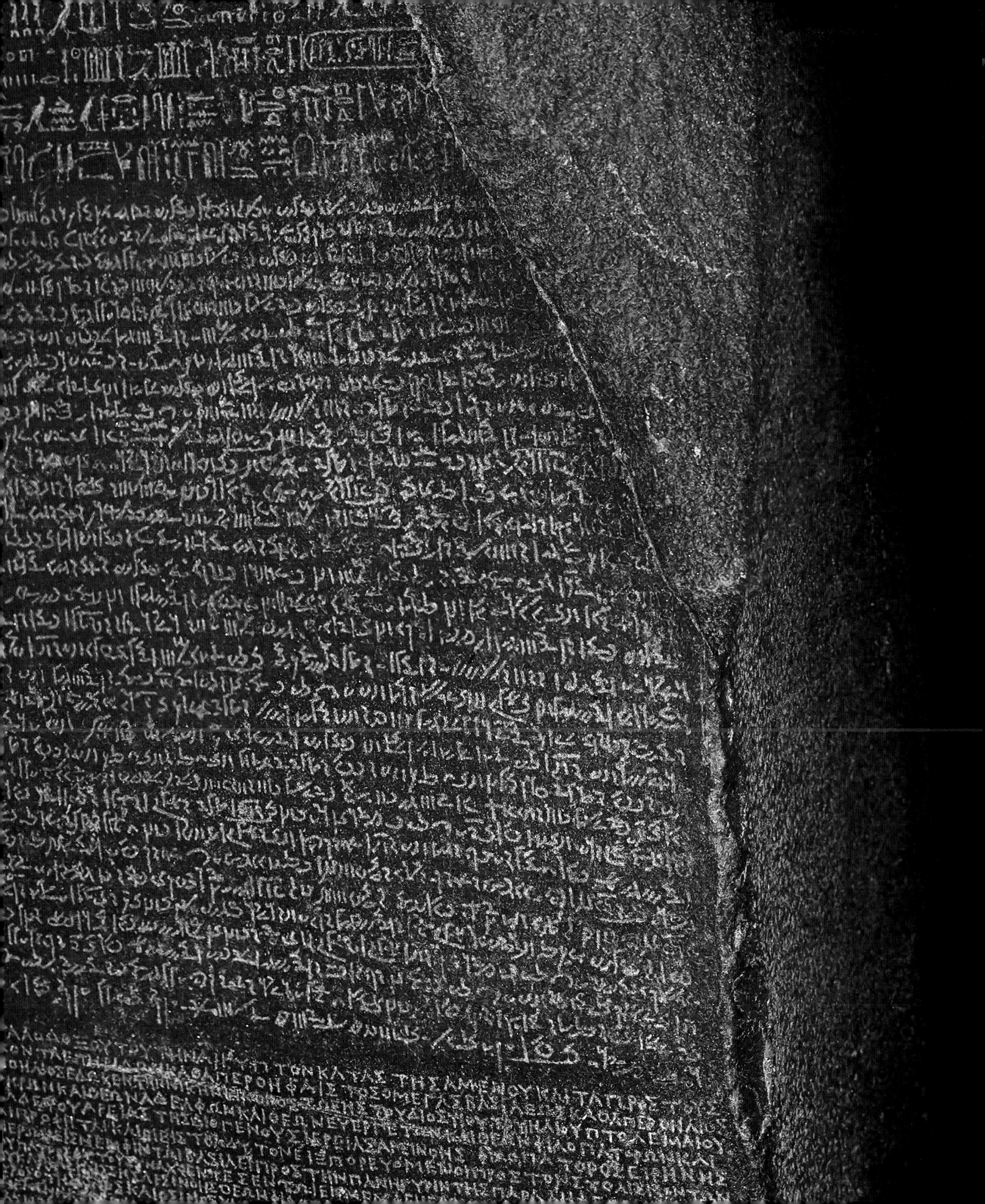

Tutankhamun's Tomb

The discovery of Tutankhamun's tomb by Howard Carter in 1922 was one of the most incredible archaeological finds ever made. Tutankhamun – who died aged just 18 – is Egypt's best-known pharaoh, though his fame is largely due to the magnificent treasures that were buried with his mummy. All the other tombs in the Valley of the Kings were robbed in ancient times. Only Tutankhamun's survived almost untouched.

ABOVE *The inner wall of Tutankhamun's tomb is carefully opened by Carter.*

The Lost Tomb

Howard Carter started working in the Valley of the Kings in 1915. All the important kings buried there had already been found, but one was still missing: Tutankhamun. Financed by Lord Carnarvon, Carter searched for four years for the "boy-king" before the rock-cut steps of a tomb were finally discovered. When Carter made a hole in the sealed doorway leading to the first room of the tomb, Lord Carnarvon impatiently asked him if he could see anything. "Wonderful things!", came the answer.

BELOW *Howard Carter inspects the golden sarcophagus containing Tutankhamun's mummy.*

RIGHT *A tiny death mask belonging to one of the two mummies of baby girls found in Tutankhamun's tomb.*

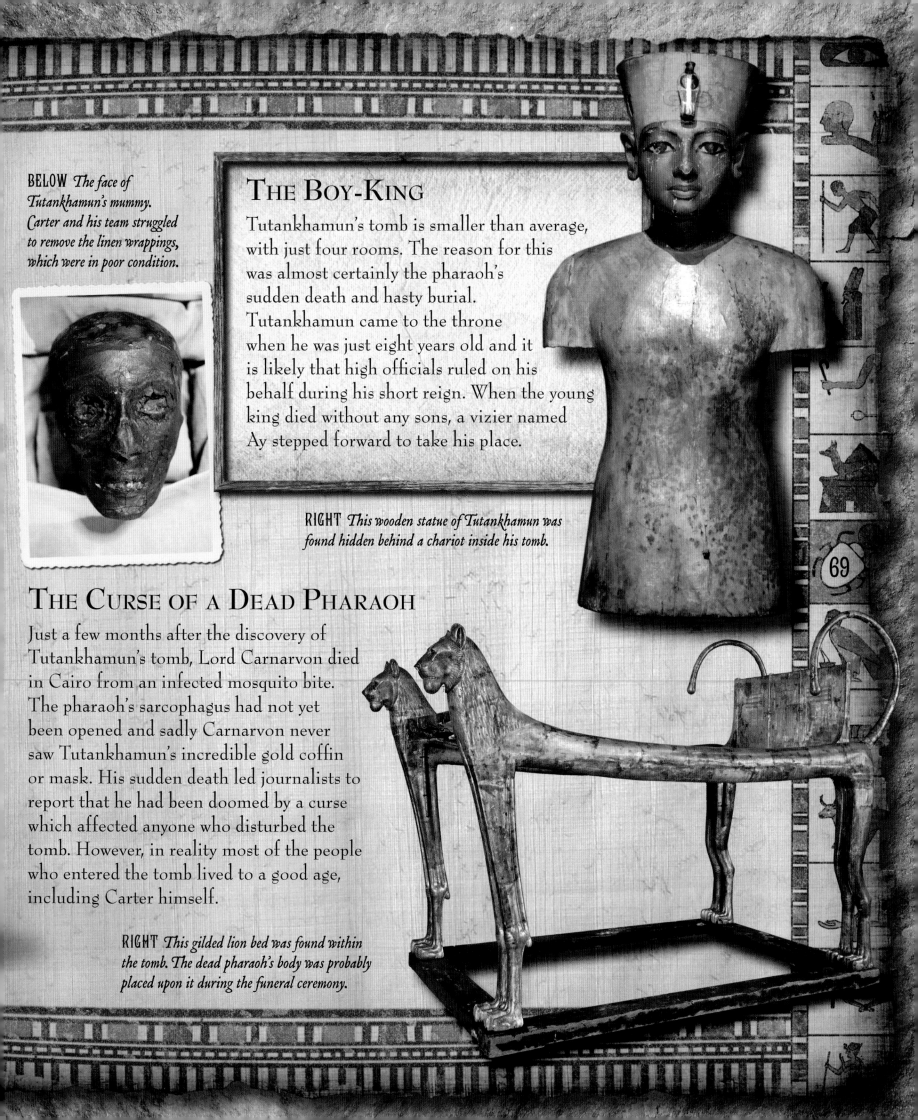

BELOW *The face of Tutankhamun's mummy. Carter and his team struggled to remove the linen wrappings, which were in poor condition.*

THE BOY-KING

Tutankhamun's tomb is smaller than average, with just four rooms. The reason for this was almost certainly the pharaoh's sudden death and hasty burial. Tutankhamun came to the throne when he was just eight years old and it is likely that high officials ruled on his behalf during his short reign. When the young king died without any sons, a vizier named Ay stepped forward to take his place.

RIGHT *This wooden statue of Tutankhamun was found hidden behind a chariot inside his tomb.*

THE CURSE OF A DEAD PHARAOH

Just a few months after the discovery of Tutankhamun's tomb, Lord Carnarvon died in Cairo from an infected mosquito bite. The pharaoh's sarcophagus had not yet been opened and sadly Carnarvon never saw Tutankhamun's incredible gold coffin or mask. His sudden death led journalists to report that he had been doomed by a curse which affected anyone who disturbed the tomb. However, in reality most of the people who entered the tomb lived to a good age, including Carter himself.

RIGHT *This gilded lion bed was found within the tomb. The dead pharaoh's body was probably placed upon it during the funeral ceremony.*

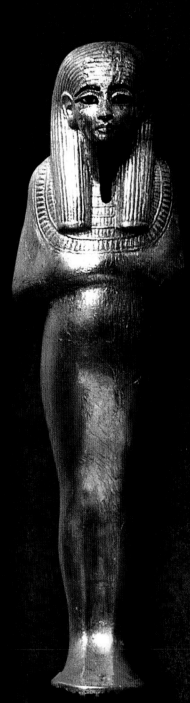

TUTANKHAMUN'S TREASURES

Tutankhamun's tomb was packed with wonderful riches, many beautifully decorated and glittering with gold. However, it was clear that robbers had twice tried to steal the tomb's precious contents – there were signs of a break-in and items had been scattered around before the thieves were apparently caught. Luckily, no serious damage was done. The treasures then survived another 3,000 years to be discovered by Howard Carter because the tomb doorway had been accidentally covered up by a mound of rubbish left by workers. After his incredible find, Carter took 10 years to record the thousands of objects inside the tomb. It is astonishing that almost 100 years later, only half of these treasures have been properly studied by experts.

LEFT *This jewelled pendant is in the form of a sacred scarab beetle.*

RIGHT *A gold-handled dagger with its ornamental sheath.*

LEFT *This ceremonial fan would have once had ostrich feathers attached around its outer edge.*

RIGHT *One of a pair of precious sandals with wooden soles and straps made of bark and gold-leaf.*

The Ramesseum

Wandering through this once-splendid temple at Thebes, I was struck by how Ramesses II had been the very image of a god-king. Here in the second courtyard, a row of crumbling figures show Osiris summoning the pharaoh back to life, while broken pieces of the king's colossal statues now lie scattered about. And somehow it seemed to me that all of Egypt's fallen greatness was contained in the eerie silence of those magnificent ruins...

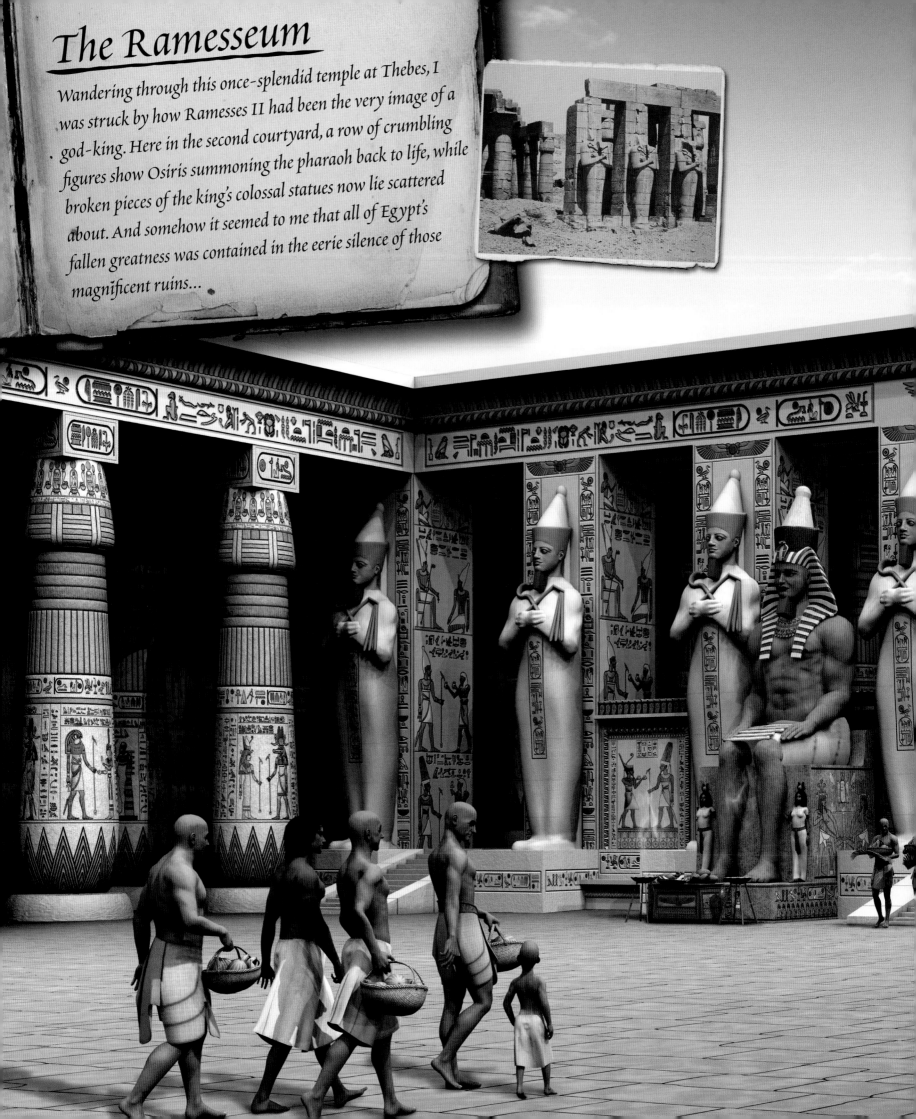

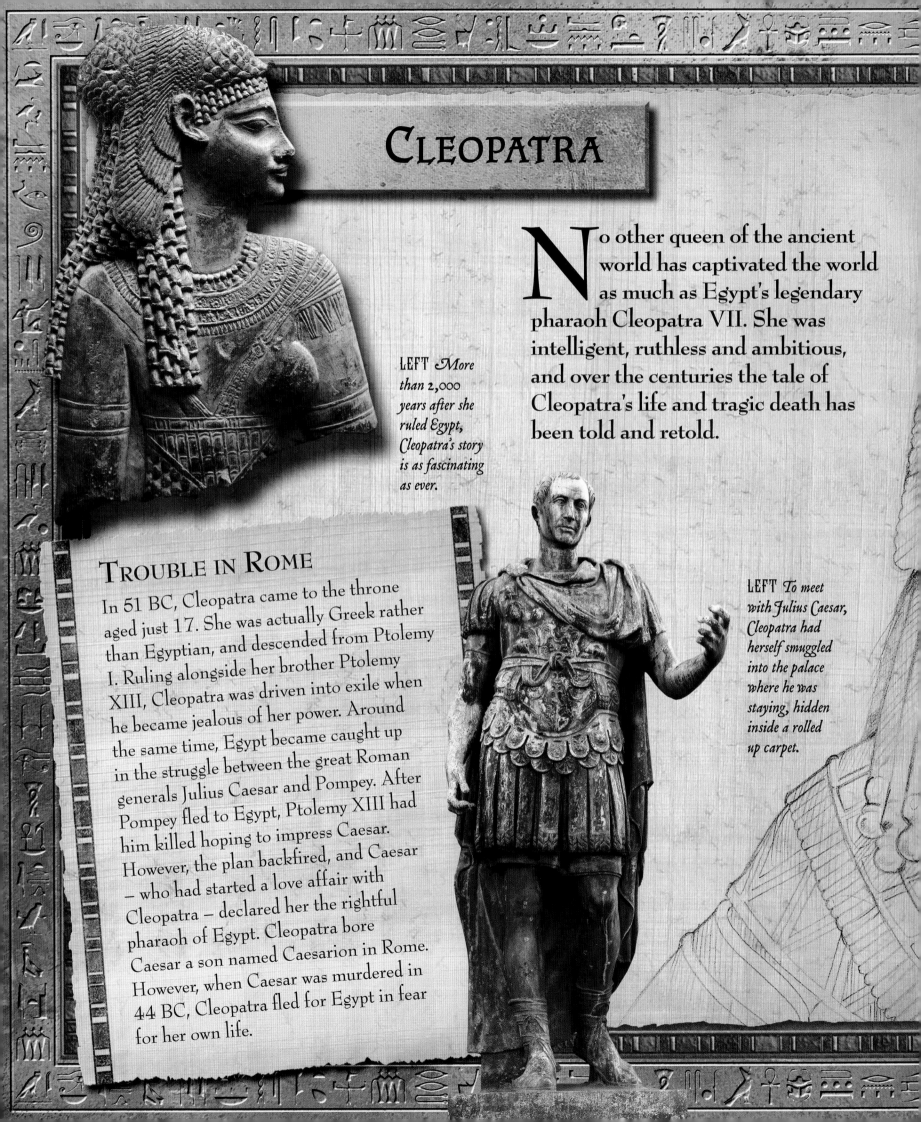

CLEOPATRA

No other queen of the ancient world has captivated the world as much as Egypt's legendary pharaoh Cleopatra VII. She was intelligent, ruthless and ambitious, and over the centuries the tale of Cleopatra's life and tragic death has been told and retold.

LEFT *More than 2,000 years after she ruled Egypt, Cleopatra's story is as fascinating as ever.*

TROUBLE IN ROME

In 51 BC, Cleopatra came to the throne aged just 17. She was actually Greek rather than Egyptian, and descended from Ptolemy I. Ruling alongside her brother Ptolemy XIII, Cleopatra was driven into exile when he became jealous of her power. Around the same time, Egypt became caught up in the struggle between the great Roman generals Julius Caesar and Pompey. After Pompey fled to Egypt, Ptolemy XIII had him killed hoping to impress Caesar. However, the plan backfired, and Caesar – who had started a love affair with Cleopatra – declared her the rightful pharaoh of Egypt. Cleopatra bore Caesar a son named Caesarion in Rome. However, when Caesar was murdered in 44 BC, Cleopatra fled for Egypt in fear for her own life.

LEFT *To meet with Julius Caesar, Cleopatra had herself smuggled into the palace where he was staying, hidden inside a rolled up carpet.*

DOOMED LOVE

In 41 BC, the Roman general Mark Antony summoned Cleopatra, believing her support would help in his struggle for power with Octavian (later the first emperor of the Roman Empire). Mark Antony immediately fell under the queen's spell and they married in 37 BC. However, their partnership was not only for love – Cleopatra was wealthy, while Mark Antony had the power to protect Egypt. In 30 BC, Mark Antony and Cleopatra took on Octavian's forces in a great sea battle at Actium off the west coast of Greece. Octavian was victorious and went on to capture Alexandria. As his soldiers deserted him, Mark Antony took his own life by falling upon his sword. Heartbroken, Cleopatra also killed herself – legend has it she was killed by the bite of an asp (a snake), but it is more likely that she took poison.

RIGHT *Mark Antony's love affair with Cleopatra ended in their tragic deaths.*

SUNKEN TREASURES

While many archaeological sites have been damaged by man, much of ancient Alexandria – the "pearl of the Mediterranean" – simply slid into the sea as a result of earthquakes in the fourth and eighth centuries BC. Since 1994, some exciting finds have been made in the waters off this ancient city.

SUBMERGED RUINS

Divers have discovered sphinxes, obelisks and even pieces of what is believed to be the Pharos of Alexandria lighthouse (one of the Seven Wonders of the Ancient World). The remains of Cleopatra's splendid palace have also been uncovered beneath the murky waves and stunning artefacts from Egypt's final dynasty continue to be brought to the surface.

Engraved for the Geographical Dictionary.

The Pharos of PTOLOMEY King of Egypt –

RIGHT *A statue of the goddess Isis, recovered from Cleopatra's sunken palace.*

LEFT *Remains of the Pharos Lighthouse were discovered on the floor of Alexandria's eastern harbour in 1994.*

LOST BENEATH THE WAVES?

The Roman historian Plutarch claimed that Mark Antony and Cleopatra were buried together in Alexandria. Perhaps their tomb has sunk beneath the ocean floor, though extensive searches have failed to uncover it. Searches have also focused around a desert temple outside Alexandria in what was once the city of Taposiris Magna. If the tomb of Egypt's famous queen is ever found, the excitement of such a discovery would surely compare to Howard Carter's unearthing of Tutankhamun.

ABOVE *The head of a statue recovered from the sea floor.*

RIGHT *A diver comes face to face with a granite sphinx.*

LEFT *This statue of Osiris was discovered in the waters off Alexandria.*

Acknowledgements

A note from the author:

When I chanced upon my great-great grandfather's journal recounting his voyage down the Nile, it stirred my imagination… And so began an enduring interest in the ancient Egyptians, a fascination that has led to the writing of this book. Many people have helped me along the way and I would like to express my gratitude to the following:

My editor Paul Virr for his guidance and helpful suggestions; the consultant John Malam for his expertise; Russell Porter and Clare Baggaley for their wonderful design work; Mark Millmore for his superb digital reconstructions; Leo Brown for his fine character drawings; Ben White for his excellent picture research; and Ena Metagic for production.

Finally I would like to pay tribute to my ancestor James Caldwell – for without his curiosity and the spirit of adventure that carried him to Egypt, this book would never have come to be.

PICTURE CREDITS

The publishers would like to thank the following sources for their kind permission to reproduce the pictures in this book.
Key: T=top, L=left, R=right, C=centre, B=bottom.

Alamy: /The Art Archive: 53bl
Art Archive: 65t, /Egyptian Museum, Cairo: 70l, /Egyptian Museum Turin/ Gianni Dagli Orti: 45b
AKG Images: /De Agostini: 32-33
Bridgeman Art Library: /De Agostini Picture Library/S. Vannini: 70c, / Egyptian Museum Cairo: 13tr, 38tr
British Museum Images: 25r (x3)
Corbis: /Bettmann: 75b, /Gianni Dagli Orti: 13tl, 71c, /Egyptian Antiquity Department: 33b, /Sandro Vannini: 6r, 35tl, 45tr, 46l, 69br, 70r, /Roger Wood: 54l, /Brian Cahn/ZUMA Press: 76-77c
Getty Images: 23b, 28b, 68bl, 68tr, /AFP: 68l, 69, 77tr, /Bridgeman Art Library: 56c, /De Agostini: 24tl, 24c, 24b, 30b, 44c, 53br, 54b, 55br, 56tl, 59b, 74tl, /Gamma-Keystone: 35c, 65r, /Science & Society Picture Library: 30tr
Griffiths Institute: 71bl
National Geographic Stock: /Kenneth Garrett: 78-79
Photo12: / Ann Ronan Picture Library: 54-55c
Reuters: 77br
Thinkstockphotos.com: 14tr, 7l, 12t, 15c, 15br, 20bl, 20tr, 22b, 26l, 46t, 46b, 47r, 53t, 57b, 57tr, 57br, 58l, 65br, 74b
Topfoto.co.uk: /Granger Collection: 27tr, 52b
Washington University (Saint Louis, Mo.) Art & Architecture Library: / Antonio Beato: 6tl, 7tc, 7tr, 9tr, 9br, 16b, 17tl, 19tl, 19br, 40b, 43b, 48b, 51tr, 51br, 60t, 63br, 63br 72t
Werman Forman Archive: Egyptian Museum Cairo: 7r, 35tr, 56l, 57l, 69br, / Louvre Museum, Paris: 7c, 46l, /Petrie Museum, University College, London: 57r, /Rupert Wace Ancient Art, London: 52t
Wiki Commons: 12b, 13br, 14b, 21br, 29r, 35br, 36-37, 65r, 66-67, 76b

Pencil art: Leo Brown © Carlton Books
CGI art: Mark Millmore © Carlton Books

Every effort has been made to acknowledge correctly and contact the source and/or copyright holder of each picture and Carlton Books Limited apologises for any unintentional errors or omissions, which will be corrected in future editions of this book.

THIS IS A CARLTON BOOK

Text, design and illustration © Carlton Books Limited 2013

Published in 2013 by Carlton Books Limited.
An imprint of the Carlton Publishing Group,
20 Mortimer Street, London W1T 3JW.

A catalogue record for this book is available from the British Library.

ISBN: 978-1-78312-009-3

Printed in Dongguan, China.